Minecraft

Master Handbook

Tony Williams

© 2015

License Notes

©Copyright by Tony Williams 2015

Disclaimer

The information provided in this book is designed to provide helpful information on the subjects discussed. The author's books are only meant to provide the reader with the basics knowledge of the topic in question, without any warranties regarding whether the reader will, or will not, be able to incorporate and apply all the information provided. Although the writer will make his best effort share her insights, the topic in question is a complex one, and each person needs a different timeframe to fully incorporate new information. Neither this book, nor any of the author's books constitute a promise that the reader will learn anything within a certain timeframe.

Table of Contents

Introduction

Are you just getting started playing Minecraft? Maybe you've been playing for a while. Whatever your situation, Minecraft has become a part of your existence. You spend your free time trying to think up new traps and buildings. That road that you put into your village doesn't look quite right. All of us have our struggles within this game.

You might see someone else's work and think that you could never attain that level of expertise. Well, think again! There are so many different ideas and possibilities within the game of Minecraft. They are just waiting to be discovered. It's your time to discover your own tricks and techniques to make your game unique and a model for other players.

What I have discovered in the time that I have spent building my Minecraft world is that there are endless possibilities. You might be working with limited resources, but the combinations that you can make with these opens the doors for whatever you can think of. Don't be afraid to use your imagination.

Another great part about Minecraft is that there are numerous web resources that will give you directions and ideas on how to implement the buildings, farms, and traps into your own game. By following the directions of others, you will be able to create your own unique creations.

While writing this book, I kept the thought of the player in mind. All of the struggles that I encountered when I first began became my focus when I put together this manual. I wanted to share the knowledge that I have acquired over the years so that someone else won't have to struggle to figure out how to do a certain task. When there's struggle, there's frustration. So, if we can limit frustration, then I hope to make players enjoy this game that much more.

Are you ready to find new ideas and tricks to making your world what you dream it could be? Then follow me as I walk you through some of the great ideas and tricks that can make you a master Minecraft guru. Not only am I going to give you tips and tricks, but I will also provide you with resources that will help you to continue your creative journey.

So, what are we waiting for? Let's take a tour of the Minecraft world and some of the tricks that master players are using! Good luck and enjoy!!!

Chapter 1

Getting Started

If you're getting started in the game of Minecraft, there are some important techniques and facts that you should keep in mind before you just jump into the game. By knowing the premise of the game, you will be better prepared to take on the challenges that it presents. People make this game a hobby. The game has spurred on many competitions for new ideas. So, without having to say it, it's a popular and competitive games.

Don't worry if you're just beginning. Even the best of the players were once beginners. Everyone has to begin somewhere. However, take the tips and techniques of the long time players to heart. They have been where you are and have learned how to make the game challenging and creative.

In this chapter, I am going to outline the basics of the game for beginners and how to start out in the game. If you're a seasoned pro, then you can either learn new techniques from this chapter or move on to the more advanced chapters. This book isn't necessarily meant to be read in order. Find what will help you and use it.

Where to Begin

If you're having trouble even knowing where to begin, then it's time to find out and get started. There are many different platforms that you can play on. The main one is the PC, but Minecraft is also available for gaming systems. So, you must figure out where you would like to play the game and get the necessary software.

I prefer to play on my PC. This offers me quick access to the internet so that I can fight other players and gather resources. I also like this because I can find advice at any time while I'm playing. Whichever method you choose to play, make sure you are comfortable with it. The game is much more enjoyable if you know your equipment and how to use it.

Setting Up an Account

Download all of the necessary software in order to play effectively. It is important that you are comfortable with the platform you are using. If you don't know how to use a gaming system, it might be better for you to download and use the software on a computer. The software can be bought and downloaded on a PC at www.Minecraft.net.

You will also be able to set up a user account on this same website. If you're not totally prepared to buy the software, the website offers a demo mode that you can play. However, in order to play the demo, you still need to register with the website. If you choose to play the demo, you have 100 hours to decide whether or not you want to continue. If so, you will be asked at that time to create a username.

The website will ask for your email and for you to create a password. It will then send you a confirmation email. After that, you are able to create a username and purchase the software. Once you have everything installed, you are ready to take on the wonderful world of Minecraft!

Creating a Profile

Once you have logged into the game using your email address and password, you are ready to begin creating your profile and start playing. By default there is one profile already set up for you in the lower left hand corner. You can play with just this profile, but it is recommended that you set up multiple profiles in order to get the maximum benefit out of your gaming experience. By having multiple profiles, you are able to play different versions of the game. Minecraft updates periodically and releases beta versions, so this might be a great option to make sure you get all the benefits of the game.

To create a new profile, simply click the "New Profile" button in the bottom left hand corner of your screen. A screen will pop up allowing you to enter the details about your profile. This will generally include a username, directory, and software version. You can create as many profiles as you like, depending on how much you want to play the game.

Creating a World

Now it's time to start actually playing! Click on the "Play" button on your screen and choose whether you would like to play a single or a multiplayer game. We are going to start a single player game, so select that option. This will take you to a screen that will show you all of the active worlds within that profile.

If you're starting a new game, your screen won't show any worlds. At the bottom, you will see a "Create New World" button. Click that. You are then able to name your new world. The automatic mode that the game is set to is survival. You are able to change that to other modes, which I will describe later in this book. If you're just a beginner, you can choose the "creative" mode so that you can easily create your world.

Click on "Create World" and let the game generate a new world for you to play in!

Playing the Game

Once you have an account set up and ready to go, you are now ready to play! In this section, I'm going to talk about the functions that you can use to move around and manipulate the world that you have just generated.

Your Inventory

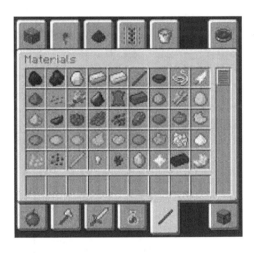

Depending on the game mode that you're playing in, you will either have an inventory or will have to search for items to add to your inventory. You can easily view your inventory by pressing E and looking through what the game mode has to offer. If you're in a game mode that doesn't give you an initial inventory, then you won't see anything within this menu.

For those modes that give you an inventory, you are able to use the supplies within it immediately. Take some time and look through your inventory and know what materials are available for your gaming use.

How to Move Around and Play

Once your new world generates, you will now be ready to move around. The game will prompt you to press the letter "E" to view your initial inventory. Depending on your game mode, these materials will differ. Make sure you know what you have in your inventory to get started.

Materials are posted along the bottom of this menu for quick access. These will probably be the materials that you will use the most. From your inventory, you are able to use anything you want in order to build. You can press your ESC key to exit this menu at any time.

Once you get a feel for the inventory, figure out what you want to build and where you would like to build it.

The game is controlled by using your keyboard. The letters of W, A, S, D, and spacebar are used to help you move through the game. W helps you to move forward, A moves you backwards, S moves you left, and D will move you right. It might take some time and experimentation to get these keys down, but once you do, you will not even have to think about it when you're playing.

The Spacebar helps you to jump. This might come in handy in certain circumstances!

Your computer's mouse controls the movement of your character's head. So, you are able to change what you're looking at by moving the mouse. Your mouse is also used to attack and smash blocks. This is done with the left mouse button. The right mouse button will let you use or set down the materials that you are holding in your hand. If you need to drop the item you're holding, you can press Q.

Try using these movements to build something. Once you're familiar with the motions, you are ready to move on in the game.

KEY OR MOUSE BUTTON	FUNCTION
W	Move forward
A	Move backward

S	Move left
D	Move right
Space bar	Jump
Right Click	Use or set down item that you're holding in your hand
Left Click	Smash what's in your hand or attack what's in front of you
Mouse Movement	Allows you to see in different directions
Scroll on Mouse	Allows you to scroll through quick access bar on in your inventory
E	Open inventory

Numbers	Allows you to scroll through the quick access inventory menu

Building Your First Item

Once you have a good feel for the game, use the materials in your inventory to build items and buildings. The different blocks have different functions, so you want to make sure that you're using blocks that are meant for building. For example, you won't want to use lava blocks for building.

I recommend that you try using granite blocks to start with. These are abundant and will allow you to build almost any structure. The first structure I built was a blacksmith building. This allowed me to control my elements to create new ones.

Stack blocks to make your structures. By doing so, you are able to generate walls and floors. Use these to create the basic structure of a building. For further reference, you can check out my eBook, *Minecraft: The Ultimate Creation Guide for Absolute Beginners to Advanced with Step by Step Directions*.

Once you have the basic functions of the game figured out, you are ready to really create your world and make things happen! As I progress through this book, I will highlight how to mine and farm, which structures are within the game, and the modes of the game. There will also be other topics, but these main ones will help with building your world one block at a time!

Chapter 2

Farming and Mining Resources

In Minecraft, using your resources to create other resources can help you to get further faster. When you begin, you are required to go and find your resources. However, it is much quicker and easier to build farms and mine your resources. This saves you time and gives you a better opportunity to build what you're working on.

What resources do you need? Well, there are numerous resources that you will encounter and be able to use in order to build whatever you wish. Some of these resources come from the Nether, while others can be farmed and mined within the Overworld. If you're just beginning, going to the Nether might not be a good plan. Finding the resources that you can build and use within your own realm will make it easier for you to get comfortable with the elements of the game.

Starting Out

We have all been there: the very beginning. It's all that we can

do to make ourselves a hut to live in and ward off attacks from others. We see others living in castles and building what we can only dream of having. Just remember, these players were once beginners too.

The first thing that you really need to get familiar with is mining ore. There are two main types of ore in this game; iron and coal. In the beginning, these are the two that we are going to concentrate on mining. After we master this, there are other types of ore such as gold, diamonds, lapis lazuli, Redstone, and emerald.

To get started out, we are going to concentrate on mining these resources so that we can use them to create other resources. In Minecraft, you initially will have to search for these resources and mine them. Let's take a look at where to find these different types of ore and how to mine them.

Coal Ore

The most abundant ore that you will find within the game is going to be coal ore. Coal ore can be mined at any elevation, so it's easy to find. Another great fact about coal ore is that it generally can be found in abundance once you find a vein. Coal ore is a great resource because it helps light your torches, cook your food, and any other activity that requires heat.

Coal ore can be mined very early on in the game and will help you to gain experience without putting yourself in danger while you're still learning the ropes. It can be mined with any pickaxe and can easily be stored to help you build up your resources.

Iron Ore

If you're looking for iron ore, you're in luck. Iron ore is the second most abundant element that you will find in the game. It can be found and mined between layers sixty-four and the bedrock layer. While you won't find it nearly as concentrated as coal ore, you are still able to find between ten to fourteen blocks at one time.

Iron ore is very useful resource in making armor, tools, and weapons. You can also use iron ore to build more advanced items such as buckets, anvils, and mining carts. It is more difficult to mine, as the iron ore must be smelted in order to get any useable material. However, it is an incredibly useful resource in your game.

Gold Ore

While both of the previous ores are found easily, gold ore is a rare resource only available in a few layers. Once found, the gold ore is only found with about four blocks of material. Like iron ore, gold ore must be smelted. It is incredibly useful for advanced techniques within the game.

Diamond Ore

Diamond ore is even rarer than gold ore. It is found within just a few deep layers within the game, but it is highly valuable and a strong resource for making weapons and tools with. You don't have to smelt diamond ore as it comes out at the time of mining.

Lapis Lazuli Ore

Lapis lazuli ore is uncommon within the game. It is found deep and in small concentrations. This ore is used mainly as a decorative accent, and it can easily be substituted by making other types of blocks blue.

Redstone Ore

Another rare ore, Redstone ore is used for many building projects. It typically is found when players are searching for diamond ore, and they accumulate it and use it later in the game. This type of ore can be used in traps and mines as well.

Redstone ore is quite useful in advanced items within the game. If found and not needed, store it for when it becomes necessary. Since it is a rare ore, you will be glad that you saved it when you did.

Emerald Ore

Emerald ore is rare. It is only found in one block increments. The uses for emerald ore are limited to it being a form of currency. So, it's probably wise not to waste a lot of time trying to mine it. If you come by it in quests and trading with villagers, be content with that.

Type of Ore	Most Common Layer	Rare Layers	None Above
Coal	128	129-131	132
Iron	64	65-67	68
Lapis Lazuli	23	31-33	33
Gold	29	31-33	34
Diamond	12	13-15	16
Redstone	15	16	17

Different Ways to Mine Resources

Just like there are many ways to come across your resources, there are also many ways to mine these resources. Depending on the area in which you are mining, a certain technique might work better than others. In this section, I am going to explain the different types of mining and how to accomplish them.

Stair Mines

A stair mine is what it sounds like: a set of stairs. Essentially, you are digging forward and down, making a stair pattern that will go down to where you're looking for resources. This is a good way to mine resources that are close to the surface, as you will probably run into them as you're digging in a stair pattern.

The downside of the stair mining method is that it can take you quickly away from your home base. Problems can result from being too far away, so you really want to stay as close to your base as you can. You can solve this problem by turning every few steps to keep your mine going down instead of going further away from where you started.

Horizontal Mines

These mines are built by going straight across rather than down. An effective way to use this method of mining is to go down and then go vertically from the main line. This will make your mine look like an antenna. By doing this, you can cover an area and go out from the main vein to look for what you're mining. You can go both deep and wide and find resources.

You can also work these mines by moving over the surface of the land. This will help you cover most of the ground and find concentrations of certain resources without searching every block. This type of mining is very effective if used correctly.

Vertical Mines

Vertical mines are not the best way to mine, but they can get you deeper faster. This type of mine is built going down in a vertical fashion. You need ladders and other tools to make sure that you can get in and out of this mine without causing you harm.

Another point of these mines is that they can be dangerous. If you go straight down, you run the risk of running into elements, such as lava and killing yourself. It is recommended that if you choose to mine in this fashion, which you build periodic ledges along the side of the mine to help protect you if something unexpected should be found beneath the surface.

Quarry Mining

A quarry mine is built by removing large areas of land, one layer at a time. If you're intent on getting all of the resources out of that area, then a quarry mine is highly effective for this. To quarry mine, you simple square off an area and dig the square. After removing all of the blocks in the first layer within the square, do the same. Keep on going down as deep as you wish in order to find what you're looking for.

Creating Farms

Farms are incredibly useful within the game, and you will find that whatever you don't want to search for can most likely be created through farming. This can be especially useful if you're playing in a mode that doesn't provide an immediate supply of resources. In this section, I am going to talk about how to set up farms and what resources can be farmed.

While farming is a good way to save time in the game, it does require resources that are gathered in the game. So, even though you are farming granite and other materials, you will still need to seek the resources necessary to build the farm.

Resources such as granite, cobblestone, obsidian and water can be produced through block generators. These are built using different resources that will mix together to create the resource. For more information on building block generators and farming materials, you can visit www.minecraftguides.org/block-generators.

Chapter 3

Tips and Tricks for Traps

Since Minecraft is a game of survival, you want to make sure that you have great traps. These can't be obvious to your enemies either. A good trap takes some time and great placement to make it work like you hope it will. This takes some time and practice, but once you have some good traps in place, you will be able to stay alive and survive longer.

A good trap has many good elements. I tend to look for suggestions from more experienced players because they have tested and tried more techniques than I have. There is a wealth of great advice and information out there. In this chapter, I am going to go through the basics of traps and give you some great resources for helping you to build your own traps.

If you don't have good traps to begin with, don't worry. Sometimes it takes a little trial and error to get something that you can use and be successful with.

Types of Traps

Traps are a great way to gain resources and ward of enemies in the game. Traps can be used for a multitude of purposes, making them a clever and easy way to accomplish your goals. In this section, I am going talk about the types of traps that can be built within the game and their purposes.

Animal Traps

Animals are a great source of food and other resources within the game. In certain modes, you need to eat and find your own resources, so knowing how to hunt and trap animals is essential to making sure you succeed. An animal trap can be a simple combination of elements or complex. It depends on the types of animals that you wish to trap. Remember, you have to retrieve whatever you have trapped, so make sure you don't get trapped within your own trap.

Enemy Traps

Again different modes within the game require you to get away from enemies. Depending on the skill level of your opponents, you might not know how to stop them using your weapons. So, in this case, building creative traps can help to insure your longevity within the game. Beware, however, that advanced players know what triggers to look for. When building a trap, you want to make it as hidden as possible.

Mob Traps

Mobs are a group of enemies that can easily destroy you if you're not prepared. Unlike an individual enemy, a mob cannot be fought off on your own. It is imperative that you have large and effective traps to either kill or catch these mobs. Most people prefer to kill their enemies. It totally depends on what your strategies and goals are.

Miscellaneous Traps

If you have a purpose for building a trap, then by all means build it! You can build traps to trap and kill. You can also build traps to get information out of your enemies. However, you really need to be aware of the consequences of a trap before building it. Some traps can be just as harmful to yourself as they are to your opponents.

Building Traps

If you're playing in a mode that requires you to survive, one of the best resources that you can have is to have traps spread around your world. It is important that you understand how traps are built and how they are going to work when triggered. The last thing that you want is to trigger a trap that you built. In this section, I'm going to discuss the types of traps and how to effectively hide them within your world.

TNT Traps

TNT traps are built with TNT somewhere in the makeup. What you are hoping for is that the player who triggers your trap will blow up. With TNT, it's total destruction, unless you have stronger materials in place around them.

A TNT trap can be very diverse, but most of them are triggered by a pressure pad that will tell the TNT when it is ready to blow. TNT can either be placed behind walls or under the floor. When the pressure pad is triggered, it will detonate the TNT and destroy whatever is within range.

The difficulty in setting a TNT trap is hiding the pressure pad so that you can take your enemy by surprise. If the other player is more experienced, it might be more difficult to hide the pressure pad because the player knows what signs in the environment to look for.

Dispenser Traps

Dispenser traps are set up to fire something at your enemy. There can be many different triggers to set off a dispenser trap, such as opening a door or stepping on a pressure pad. When you set up a dispenser trap, you want to make sure that the trigger is concealed so that you can take your opponent by surprise. Dispenser traps are basically a series of elements that add up for the big reveal.

For more information on how to build traps, you can refer to www.minecraftguides.org. This website has a wide variety of how to manuals that will help you in building whatever you wish to build.

Once you are familiar with traps and how to build them, you can get creative and start to build your own. Knowing how certain elements will react with one another will make it easier for you to build and design effective traps to ensure your survival in Minecraft.

Tips for Building a Great Trap

Once you have some ideas for building traps, take a few moments to see if they meet the criteria below:

-Does it perform the functions you want it to?

Take a look at the complete set up of your trap. If someone was going to walk into this trap, will it do what you intended for it to? If it doesn't, then you need to make adjustments to it in order to ensure that it will be successful when it needs to work

-Is it well hidden?

A good way to make sure that your trap is successful is that it is out of view from its victim. If a player knows that there has been a trap set for him or her, they will either try to trigger it to make it detonate or they will avoid it altogether. Either way, your trap did not perform the way that you intended for it to.

-Will it destroy something you don't want it to?

If your trap will destroy your buildings or other items that you don't want damaged, you need to either rethink the trap or place your trap in a location where it won't damage the items you want to keep safe. TNT traps are especially destructive, so really think through your placement of the trap before you set it up and want it to work.

-Do you intend to reuse it?

Some traps can be retriggered to work more than once. However, if you're using explosives, don't expect to use those again. If you want the trap to repeat its function over and over, then make sure you find a way to make that happen. It might be set on a clock or other device that can time its ability to restore itself and work again.

Think through your trap. Don't be hasty and set up traps that can hurt you or destroy your resources. Traps are meant to serve a purpose, whether it be to kill your enemies or to trap them. Evaluate what you wish for your traps to do and build them accordingly. It can save you both time and resources!

Chapter 4

Knowing the Structures and Biomes in Minecraft

The game of Minecraft features many diverse structures. Some seem pretty self-explanatory, such as houses, but there are some structures that you will find that will leave you wondering what they are. Once you understand the structures in the game, you will be better able to build them within your own game. As with everything else, structures will require resources, but I will cover some of the resources that are necessary to be used within a structure.

The more structures that you have, the better. Structures are good for hiding traps in. The more complex the structure, the higher the likelihood that you can install traps that will take the most experienced players by surprise. So, let's take a look at some of the structures in the game and how you can use them to your advantage.

When starting out in a world, there will be no structures. It is like landing in the middle of an undiscovered wilderness. It is up to you to build and develop it and make it into your own vision. Structures can be anything from physical buildings to landmarks. Once you know what you're capable of creating, the possibilities are endless!

Types of Structures

With building structures within your game, the sky is the limit. Whatever you would like to build, you can build it. You will just need to find the necessary resources and take the time to build the structure. Depending on the mode that you're playing in, you will have more time and resources in some than others.

I recommend that you build necessary structures first, then worry about the decorative ones. You don't want to use up your resources on building unnecessary structures and not having enough to build what you need. Assess your inventory and decide what you need most and how to build it.

However, even though most of the structures that you will encounter will be built by you, there are still some that can be found while exploring. These structures can be incredibly dangerous, but they can also generate riches and resources. Depending on the location and the structure, the possibilities of what you will find differ. Along with the types of structures you can build on your own, I am also going to outline some of the structures that you can find while exploring within your world.

Villages

Villages are important structures to have. The people who inhabit your villages are useful to trade with, buy resources from, and get help from if you need it. The villagers are non-players, so they are not considered enemies, but a resource. Depending on your gaming style, you can either be on friendly terms with your villagers or you can raid and pillage the villages.

Structures that are useful to you within a village are blacksmith shops, butcher shops, and farms. These will provide you with food and resources to help you survive during the game. Other resources can be traded for and taken from villagers.

A village typically consists of at least four buildings and a well. The buildings can either be built by villagers or you can provide villages for the people. Whatever your plans are for your game, you can decide what needs to be built and what can wait for others to develop.

Desert Temples

If your world has deserts within it, you can probably find desert temples. Desert temples are pyramid-shaped abandoned structures that have a basement which more than likely houses treasure as well as danger. Many desert temples have underground rooms that have explosives within them.

So, when you encounter a desert temple, you need to weigh the costs versus the benefits. You can easily set off the traps within the underground room, or you can find great wealth stored within it. You are the one who needs to determine whether or not that is a risk you're willing to take.

Witch Huts

Witch huts can develop in jungle and plain biomes. These are simple structures that can spawn witches. Witches are dangerous non-player characters, so approach these structures with caution. No resources can be found within these structures, so if you're a new player, it might be best to avoid these altogether.

Jungle Temples

Much like the desert temples, jungle temples are structures that are abandoned within the jungle biome. They are like the desert temples that I have described above. These structures are rigged with traps, so if you go into them to look for treasures, be aware of this. The last thing that you want is to be blown up or trapped because you became greedy. Know what you're prepared to encounter. If you're an inexperienced player, it might be best to avoid until you know you can handle what is within.

Dungeons

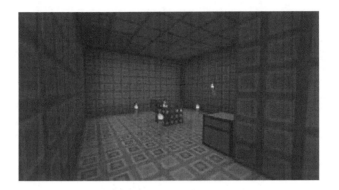

A dungeon is a small underground room in the game of Minecraft. You can happen upon these if you're traveling through abandoned mineshafts. What is unique about dungeons is that each one of them comes with one or two chests that can be looted for resources. The downside of the dungeons are that there is a monster spawner in each one. Be aware of this if you're within a dungeon.

You can either destroy or try to farm the spawner. A monster spawner can be a source of great resources, so think before you destroy.

Abandoned Mineshafts

Finding an abandoned mineshaft can be a tremendous opportunity for you. Abandoned mineshafts were built and then abandoned for some reason or another. Someone was mining and left resources down in these tunnels. In an abandoned mineshaft, you can find a lot of valuable resources. In chests, you can find food and loot. Fence posts and rails can be taken for your own use. In some mineshafts, you can even find exposed veins of resources.

Abandoned mineshafts are wonderful because a lot of the work is already done for you. All you have to do is mine the ore. It's like free money, so to speak.

Even if you're not looking for resources, abandoned mineshafts can be used to travel into the depths. This can be useful if you're trying to ditch enemies and don't want to be seen. Whatever your reasoning for traveling the abandoned mineshaft, it is a great resource that should be looked upon fondly.

Strongholds

Strongholds are extremely rare and even rarer to just find within your world. Only a few are in each world, so when you find one, you know you got lucky.

These are underground fortresses that closely resemble castles. You can only find them with a few ways. One of the ways to happen upon one would be the abandoned mineshafts. These can intersect with a stronghold, even though it is rare. Ravines and caverns are other ways that you can find a stronghold. The final way to find one of these is to use the Eye of Ender tool. This is a game end tool, so it's unlikely that you will be able to use this method.

Why are strongholds rare and why are they worth finding? Well, strongholds hold a plethora of wealth. You can find resources, books, and other valuable things within these rooms. They can also serve as an underground home base. This can make it difficult for others to seek you out. This structure also hold a Portal Room, which will allow you to go to the End Realm and fight the Ender Dragon.

Beaches

Beaches are a structure that you can build on your own accord. By using your resources and your creativity, you can create a fantastic beach near the water's edge. Be creative and let your world look the way that you would like it to. With the resources that are available within the game, you can build anything you can possibly imagine.

Seaports

Seaports are another structure that can be built within the game. If you want to have a shipyard, this can really give your world a definite nautical quality. This too can be built at the edge of the water by putting in huts, docks, and even lighthouses.

Houses

Having a house to call your home base is a good idea. You can build whatever type of home you like. Your home can be used for storing materials, food, and other resources that you cannot take along with you when you travel. It is also a place you can use to recover when you're not playing the game.

Structures can come in very handy within the game. Whether you are building them for decoration or seeking them out for resources, by knowing what to expect out of your structures ensures the you won't walk into a trap or something else unexpected. Your game mode will also affect which structures will appear in your world. When you create a world, it comes with some of each of these and you are able to build others. It all depends on what your game plan is and how you plan to use them.

Chapter 5
Surviving Minecraft

Minecraft is based on survival. However, surviving in the game can be quite difficult if you are new. The best way that you can insure your survival is to know what to expect and how to protect yourself while you're building and expanding. As I've stated before, everyone has been a beginner. So, why not take some advice from those who have been there?

Survival methods are different as you progress in your game. The more experienced you are, the higher the likelihood that you will be attacked. With that said, there are also just as many ways to protect yourself. In this chapter, I'm going to provide some tips and tricks for survival at all experience levels. No matter where you are now, there is something that can help you survive.

Survival Mode

Even though I'm going to go into more detail about game modes

in the next chapter, I really wanted to go into more detail about

the most popular mode within the game. Survival mode is the

default mode and the most played. However, if you're new to

the game, survival mode can be extremely difficult for you to

survive even one night.

Other players are out on a mission too. They will take

opportunities to kill and loot your supplies. With that fact being

said, I want to give you some tips as to how to survive in survival

mode. I recommend that if you're new to the game that you try

your hand in the safer modes first. Once you have a good feel

for the game, then take a stab at surviving in survival mode.

Characteristics of Survival Mode

Survival mode in Minecraft is much like the reality television

show "Survivor." You are essentially put into a habitat with

40

nothing and are expected to make due for yourself with whatever resources happen to be left lying around. Whatever you eat, wherever you sleep, and whatever you encounter has to be dealt with as it comes. On top of all this, there are mobs that are out to get you.

When you are dropped into a biome in Survival Mode, you have nothing. You have no inventory, no home base, and no food. So, you have to learn how to provide for yourself. You also have to protect yourself.

Finding Food and Shelter

The first thing that you will want to accomplish is to find a source for food and for shelter. Without any tools, you will have to eat what is naturally growing within the biome that you're in. This can be difficult if you land in a desert, but not impossible.

Finding shelter may be a little more difficult. If you're in an area that has caves or other natural structures, you're set. Another way that you can create a shelter is by using the trees that are available, if there are any. You can obtain wood initially by punching the tree. Once you have enough wood, you can build a structure that can serve as temporary shelter.

Use your resources. Sometimes you're going to have to think outside the box in order to find a solution to these two basic needs.

Finding Resources

The next step that you will want to worry about is finding the resources necessary to make tools and weapons. The first tool will be a wooden pickaxe that will assist you in finding stone to upgrade your tools. By using a pickaxe, you are now able to begin mining for other resources to build within your biome.

Some resources require stronger tools, so you may have to mine and work your way up to the different types of ores that are mined within the game. You will also need to find a source to smelt the ores that require smelting.

Once you have some resources in your inventory, it's time to work on setting up buildings and traps to help ward off the mobs that will come after you.

Mobs

In the Minecraft world, anything that travels in a pack is considered a mob. Therefore, even animals are considered mobs. Mobs have many types in this game. Some will help you and some will kill you. So, let's figure out the difference so that you don't die by approaching a mob!

Passive Mobs

These mobs are the animals in the game that will never attack you. Animals that are considered passive mobs include pigs, sheep, cows, chickens, mushrooms, horses, ocelots, bats, squid, and villagers. The animals in this type of mob can be spawned to create more of the resource. This is useful when using them as a food resource. However, they will only spawn in certain conditions, so look at that before you start farming animals.

Cows, sheep, pigs, and horses spawn on grassy and forested land in small herds. Think farm animals. They like to be where there is sun and grass. These animals can be butchered for meat or cows can also be used to gain milk. Players like to fence these in so that they will have infinite resources for food.

-Chickens are spawned by throwing eggs. In midair, the egg will hatch and turn into a chicken. Chickens produce eggs and are good for food as well. You can produce one serving of chicken by killing a chicken. If left alive, the chickens will continue to produce eggs.

-Cows produce milk and food as well. When killing a cow, you get around one to three servings of beef. If left alive, they will continue to produce milk. Cows will also produce leather when killed, which is another great resource for your inventory.

-Mushrooms are the cows of the mushroom biome. They produce the same resources as a cow, just in a different environment. Mushrooms also produce mushroom stew when killed. These mobs are considered the most versatile animals within the entire game.

-Horses are great because they can provide transportation and carry items. They don't produce much in the way of food or resources, so taming a horse and using it for transportation would serve you better than anything else.

-Ocelots are wild cats that can be found in the jungle biome. You can tame one of these cats by using wild fish. Once tamed, they will follow around the player. They are good at defending you against Creepers.

-Bats are a pretty much useless animal in the game. They will not harm you and don't have any good characteristics that will help you. The only thing that they can be good for is to give you a hint as to where underground caverns are located, as they make a lot of noise.

-Squids can be killed in order to obtain ink, which can be used in crafting more advanced Minecraft items, such as books and quills.

-Villagers are the mobs that inhabit your villages. They are good for trading and doing business with. Or, if you're the seek and destroy type, you can pillage their villages for your own personal gain.

Utility Mobs

Utility mobs consist of iron golems and snow golems. These mobs are used to help the player in the quest. Both of these can be created by the player, while only one will occur naturally.

The Iron Golem protects villages. You can find them naturally or build one yourself using four iron blocks with a pumpkin placed on top. Iron Golems are also found in villages where there at least ten villagers and twenty one houses. So, if you attack a village that has an Iron Golem, it will try and prevent you from taking over.

The Snow Golem doesn't occur naturally, but has to be spawned by the player. Essentially, you stack to blocks of snow with a pumpkin on top. You then have a little snowman that throws snowballs at hostile mobs. This type of golem can be used for protection if you are in the snow biome.

Neutral Mobs

Neutral mobs share a lot of the characteristics of the passive mobs. However, the difference between the two mobs is that a neutral mob will counterattack if provoked. A passive mob will let you beat on it, but a neutral mob will fight back. The different mobs in this category are provoked in different ways. In this category are wolves, spiders, cave spiders, Endermen, and zombie pigmen.

Each of these mobs can spawn in different biomes and will attack you if you provoke them. So, if you don't want confrontation, don't provoke them!

-Wolves are found in forest and taiga biomes. You can provoke a wolf only by hitting it. When you hit one wolf, you will get attacked by the entire pack of wolves. You can tame wolves and turn them into dogs, which will go into battle with you. All you have to do to tame a dog is give it a bone.

-Spiders and Cave Spiders are neutral only in daylight. If you come across spiders in low light, they will attack you because they become aggressive mobs. They can be poisonous and overwhelm an unsuspecting player. However, when killed, spiders will produce string and spider eyes.

-Endermen are tall dark creatures that spawn in the Overworld and the End. They can be provoked by attack or by looking at them. So, if you see them, try not to provoke an attack by looking at them. When killed, the Endermen will drop End Pearls, a necessary resource to get to the end of the game.

-Zombie Pigmen spawn when lightning strikes near a herd of pigs. They are only aggressive if attacked and will attack in groups. When killed, they produce rotten flesh and gold nuggets. They are rarely seen in the Overworld, but are common in the Nether.

By knowing what will provoke each of these mobs will help you to either avoid or destroy them when you encounter them. It all depends on your game plan what you choose to do with these mobs.

Aggressive Mobs

These mobs are exactly as they are described: aggressive. You don't have to do anything to them for them to come after you.

They don't like anyone and will attack anyone. The mobs in this category include zombies, creepers, skeletons, slimes, silverfish, and witches. These are the guys that will kill you in survival mode. So, if you see one, prepare for a fight or prepare to run. It all depends on how prepared you are to take on an aggressive mob.

-Zombies come to life when it's dark. You will encounter them commonly in caves. They move about, making noise, in order to find villagers or players to eat. Zombies are sensitive to daylight and will die when exposed to it. When killed, zombies can produce a bunch of different resources. You don't know what you will find when killing one.

-Creepers get their name by sneaking up on players and blowing up like a bomb. These creatures are small with four legs and make very little noise. When they blow up, they can cause significant damage to whatever they are near. If you should kill a creeper before it blows up, it will give you gunpowder. Like all the other aggressive mobs, they spawn in darkness, but sunlight will not kill them.

-Skeletons are sensitive to sunlight and will provide you with bones to tame wolves with when killed. They carry a bow and are very aggressive. Sometimes, you can get their bow from them when killing them. They will fire their arrows when they get close enough to a player and are great at navigating any incline to get to a player.

-Slimes are slow and easy to kill. When attacked, they will break into smaller cubes. When killing a slime, they produce slime that can be useful in creating sticky pistons and leads for animals. They are commonly found in caves and jungles.

-Silverfish are mobs that are found in Strongholds and in the Extreme Hills biome. They are extremely rare and a player can play for years without running into one.

-Witches are dangerous mobs that spawn in the Overworld. They attack the players by throwing potions at them. Even though they are nasty creatures, if you should kill one, they can give you a large amount of loot. The materials that they drop can be quite rare, so it might be worth it to attack and defeat a witch.

Aggressive mobs can be a pain in the rear, but they can produce resources that will make it worth the effort to fight them. By knowing their characteristics and how they attack, you will be better prepared to protect yourself against these mobs if you should encounter them.

By knowing what you will encounter as threats in the game will help you prepare better to be able to survive, no matter what you skill level is. When encountering the challenges and animals in the game, you will be able to know what can possible present a threat to you and what it relatively harmless. Once you feel more prepared, attacking and taming some of the creatures in mobs can be a great resource for you when making your way through the game.

Chapter 6

Minecraft's Game Modes and Themes

When you see people talk about Minecraft, you hear them mainly talk about one of its modes. The survival mode is the most popular mode within the game. However, there are other modes within Minecraft that can be played. If you're more of a creative person, then you don't have to fight. There is a mode for every kind of player!

In this chapter, we are going to outline the modes of Minecraft, along with a few themes that might interest you when you're building in the game. I will also provide resources that you can use to spark your own imagination and get your gaming to the level you want it!

Gaming Modes

When starting out your game of Minecraft, you have a few options on how you wish to play. If you just want to get a feel for the game, you might not want to start out in a survival mode. Learning to build and gain resources is valuable when learning how to play. Take on whichever mode will help you best to gain the experience you need to play the game.

Survival Mode

I talked a little about surviving within survival mode in the last chapter. However, there is more to survival mode than just the dangers and the mobs that inhabit it. The nice thing about Survival Mode is that you are able to choose the level of difficulty of the game. So, if you're not quite ready to have a hard game, you can make Survival Mode easier until you feel more skilled.

When beginning your game, you will have the choice of which mode you wish to play in. The game is automatically set to Survival Mode, as it is the most popular mode in the game. Survival mode has several characteristics that make it live up to its name. In survival mode, you are essentially dropped into a random biome and are responsible for keeping yourself alive.

In Survival Mode, you start with nothing but the environment around you. Once there, you have to find the necessities to keep you alive and help you to thrive. Food, shelter, weaponry, and anything else that you could possibly need must be obtained by you in some manner.

Not only do you start with absolutely nothing, but there are mobs that are likely to attack you when they see you. Taking on the mobs can either be an easy or a difficult job, depending on the mob and your skill level. In the last chapter, I discussed the mobs and their characteristics. Some of the mobs can be a great resource, while others are best avoided until you have weaponry. Once you have the hang of farming, mining and building, you can gradually increase the difficulty of the game so that you feel more challenged.

Many people enjoy the challenge that the Survival Mode offers, and that is why it is the most popular gaming mode. However, if you're not into survival, there is still a mode in Minecraft that may be appealing to you.

Creative Mode

Creative Mode gives you the opportunity to create and make your game into whatever you want it to be. You are the creator of this world, so you can do anything that you wish with it. This can be appealing to players who don't appreciate being attacked by mobs.

In Creative Mode, you are provided with everything you could possibly need at the start of the game. When you open your inventory, you will find all of the resources already available. You don't have to worry about hunting and mining for the materials that you will need to create what you're imagining.

This is a great mode to build a dream world. You will have no opposition, so you won't have to worry about fighting off mobs or running into traps. Since you already have all the materials, all you have to do is put them together to make buildings and other things.

Hardcore Mode

Hardcore mode is basically survival mode at its toughest. On this setting, it's like setting yourself on Survival Mode at the top of its difficulty.

For this game mode, you really need to be prepared in order to survive. The attacks will be more aggressive, resources will be harder to find, and it will all start the moment you land in your game. If you know what to expect, you stand a better chance at surviving in this mode.

Be prepared to have little peace. The mobs are going to be out to get you and you're going to have to think fast and act quickly.

The Biomes of the Game

We have talked about biomes throughout this book. I would now like to outline the biomes that are commonly found in the game of Minecraft and some of the features of each. If you should land in one of these biomes, you will be better prepared to find resources and search for materials.

Lush Biomes

The lush biomes of the game include the grassy fields and thick forests that you will most likely see advertising the game. Other biomes that are included in this category would be jungles and swamps. A lush biome is any biome that has thick growth.

-Grasslands-These areas are fields covered with tall and flowing grasses. As mentioned in previous chapters, they often spawn the farm type animals and can be used for farming for other resources. While many of the structures that we have outlined typically occur here, these are areas where you will typically see villages form.

-Forests- Forests are trees that are placed closely together. Depending on the forest, you might have trees so closely growing together that you cannot see the forest floor or the forest floor might be covered in flowers. You can find random structures in these forests. Approach structures with caution to avoid being taken by surprise by mobs or traps.

-Jungles- These biomes are a different type of forest. The trees are tropical and there are different types of structures that can occur here. Learning about what can be found in the jungle biome is beneficial to making sure you can survive in this biome if you should drop in there.

-Swamps- This biome is made up of swamp land. It is heavy in vegetation. The trees often resemble those of a normal forest.

Cold Biomes

Cold biomes are areas where the temperature is cold and finding vegetation can be found but difficult to use as a resource. They are modeled after the steppe climate that is commonly found in Eastern Europe and Western Russia. In this biome, you will find biome steep mountain ranges that will rise high into the clouds. Since there are plentiful mountains, the caves are also numerous. If dropped one of these locations, you will have an easier time mining for resources and finding caves to mine.

-The Extreme Hills biome is a cold biome that is rich in coal resources. Since coal is a necessary resource in the game, finding yourself in this biome could be to your benefit.

-Taiga Forests- the cold biomes also feature taiga forests, which consists of larger trees that are found in colder climates. There are also Great Taiga forests that have even taller trees. This biome offers a supply of mossy rock that usually can only found in structures in the game.

Cold biomes offer a wide array of resources that cannot be found anywhere else in the game. If you want to find an abundance of mossy rock, the highest concentrations of this resource are found in the cold biomes.

Snowy Biomes

Snowy Biomes are much like Cold Biomes except that they boast snow and lots of it. Here you can find mobs that do not exist in other biomes. These biomes also provide snow storms. A snowy biome will not harm the player. However, the resources might be limited.

-Snowy Plains- the snowy plains biome is much like the grassy plains biome except that it is covered in snow. Frequent snow storms cover the ground with a blanket of snow. If you live in areas that experience snow in the winter time, then this biome is much like what you would experience during a typical winter. The water features are frozen over and you cannot find green vegetation growing on the ground.

-Cold Taiga- Cold Taiga mirrors the regular taiga found within the game. In this biome, you will find tall trees and steep hills. However, instead of it being a lush biome, you will find that it is cold and winter-like.

Snowy Biomes show the seasons within the game. If you should happen to drop into one of these, there are a few features and structures that are not found anywhere else in the game, including ice peaks that can be made into forts. If you're a winter enthusiast, you will enjoy falling in on one of these cold and snowy biomes.

Dry Biomes

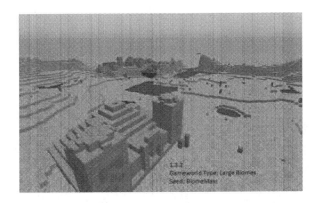

Unlike the Lush Biomes, Dry Biomes are pretty much barren of green vegetation. The climate is so dry in these areas that there is little to no vegetation growth. The dry biomes boast lots of sand. So, it's natural to say that the desert biome is going to fall into this category.

While you cannot find much in the way of vegetation or precipitation, you can still find villages and the Desert Temples that we spoke of in a previous chapter. These are great resources for finding food and shelter. However, you can still encounter hostile mobs, so be aware of this if you should fall into this biome.

-Savannah Biomes- Savannahs are also part of this biome. They are a dry climate that has few trees and limited vegetation. If you have ever been to Africa, this biome is a great example of what you will find.

-Mesa Biomes- Mesa biomes are known for clay resources. While it is possible to farm clay from river beds, finding it in a Mesa Biome will make the job easier and you will find more of the resource, which means that you will waste less time trying to find it in river beds.

The Dry Biomes have elements that are just as useful to the player as what they would find in a grassy biome. If you have ever traveled the world, you will appreciate the differences in temperature, scenery, and climate. Also, the creative possibilities for these biomes challenge you to new projects wherever you should end up within the game.

Ocean Biomes

Ocean biomes are found near large bodies of water. Like their name, you will find a lot of ocean within this biome. Ocean biomes also boast a different type of vegetation and animal population. By using the resources found in the water, you can gain items such as ink from the squids.

In this category of biome, there are two distinct varieties. The regular ocean biome has water that is minimally deep while the deep ocean biome has water that is twice as deep. When looking at these, you will not be able to tell them apart right away.

Ocean biomes boast islands. Depending on where you are, islands can be numerous or there could only be a small island. By learning the resources that can be mined from the ocean biomes, you can figure out a way to survive them, no matter what is given at the beginning of the game.

All of these biomes are as different and vast as the next. The great part about this game is that you will not see the same setup for the same biome twice. Every time a world is generated, the biomes will have different elements to them. They will look the same vegetation wise, but the vegetation and the structures will occur in different places with different quantities

Even though you will not know what to expect out of an individual game, knowing the characteristics of the type of biome will make your adventure different than any of the ones you have been on before.

Knowing What Biome You are In

If you land in an area that you cannot identify the game has a feature that will tell you what biome you are currently in. Some biomes will be well pronounced while others will have you scratching you head, wondering where you are and what you're supposed to do.

Try hitting the F3 key. This will bring up text detailing the specifications of the land. If you look towards the bottom, you can see the type of biome that the game has generated for you. Once you know that, you are ready to get started in finding resources and building a home base.

Themes of the Game

Themes within your game can be entirely up to you. I have seen people have Viking Themes, cartoon themes, and any other type of theme under the sun. When you get started with the game, look at the biome around you. Most of the time, an idea for a theme will pop out for you and you will be able to design and make that theme work in multiple ways.

Using your supplies and resources can offer a creative outlet that will help you explore and build. Whether you are playing in creative or survival mode, there will always be a need to build and design structures. So, why not make it fun and interesting by applying a theme to it?

Looking on the internet, I have seen tons of awesome buildings and landscapes that I wish I would have thought of first. If you have an idea welling up in you, then by all means, try it!!! You might be glad that you did!

Knowing which game mode and the characteristics of your biome can be essential to your survival. Sure, you can wing it, but if you are serious about surviving Minecraft, you will understand where you are and what you must do to survive. If you're in a game mode that doesn't require survival, knowing your biome will help you in your creative exploits. The more you know, the further that you can go in your game!

Additional Resources

Great resources can be found for mining and farming throughout the internet. Don't be afraid to use YouTube and internet search engines to find what you're looking for. There are also many blogs and forums on the internet that will give you hints and pointers for making and using almost everything that you will find in the game.

Even though mining is more of a necessity in some modes than others, it is still helpful to know where to find and mine elements. I like to use the farming techniques to set up farms for my resources that would be a waste of time to search for. That way, I can spend time looking for resources that I actually need. New things are being discovered all the time, so if you find something, share it with the gaming community online!

Some of the resources that I have found that will help new and aspiring players are on the internet as well as in other eBooks that I have encountered. I will supply a list of each that will get you going.

Internet Resources

www.minecraftguides.org

This site offers expansive resources for building and mining resources. It also offers ideas unique to the websites administrator that will get your creative juices flowing. If you struggle with the mechanics of building items in the game, this is a great tutorial site for you to look through. It features numerous pictures of what the author talks about.

www.youtube.com

As with almost every other task in the world, YouTube boasts a great video library of methods and tutorials for Minecraft players of all skill levels. Whatever you're setting out to do, you can type it into the search on YouTube and find a tutorial video. Some videos are of excellent quality while others are a waste of time. User ratings will give you a good indication of this.

www.howtogeek.com/school/htg-guide-to-minecraft

This site offers information on the game and walks you through a game from start to finish. It provides pictures and instructions on how to perform certain tasks and how to obtain necessary resources.

Book Resources

Minecraft: The Ultimate Creations Guide, for absolute Beginners to Advanced, Simple step by Step

You can also browse through the offerings on www.amazon.com to find Minecraft books that would be helpful to your game. Remember, check the user ratings before purchasing them so that you don't waste your money.

Conclusion

Minecraft is one of the most popular games being played today. With this much attention, it must be a captivating and exciting game to many. From its diverse game modes to its unexpected elements, Minecraft is a game that you will not encounter the same challenges twice. With this type of adventure, you're sure to get addicted to the game and all of its elements. Whether you enjoy the challenge of survival or the challenge of creativity, Minecraft has a way to captivate you.

Many people are intimidated by this game due to its diverse nature. However, there isn't anything to fear. Just because it's a game that will never be cookie-cutter consistent doesn't make it a game to avoid. Look at this game as an adventure and use it as such.

In this book, we have covered a wide array of information and resources that can be helpful to players of any skill level. I believe that it is important to know and understand the game in order to achieve what you want with it. So, I have provided information on the different biomes, mobs, resources, and traps that can be used in the game. I have also given you some instructions on how to obtain resources through mining, farming, and killing mobs.

Whatever your skill level, you can find out more. By all means, this book isn't an all-inclusive guide to the game, so I recommend that you seek other resources to help you in your quest. Every player will have a different design and a different goal. So, you must find the resources that will help you achieve what you want from the game.

With an initial understanding of the game, you can grow and become a much better player quickly. I know that when I first picked up the game, I was totally overwhelmed and lost. This game was asking me to fend for myself? How in the world did I do that? I couldn't even figure out how to move!

Take some time and get to know this game and all of its elements. You will be glad that you did! If you should find more helpful methods and tips, I urge you to go onto a forum and share them with others. Everyone who is serious about this game will enjoy a fresh take on the game!

Finally, I just want to wish you good luck and I hope that you get what you're looking for out of this game. With each new adventure, you will grow as a player and help those who are new and old alike learn the concepts of this game and how much fun it can be for all!

Made in the USA
Lexington, KY
27 July 2015